SOUTHWEST OF ITALY

Stanzas for a Travel Memoir

GUERNICA WORLD EDITIONS 55

SOUTHWEST OF ITALY

STANZAS FOR A TRAVEL MEMOIR

FEDERICO PACCHIONI

GUERNICA
World
EDITIONS

TORONTO—CHICAGO—BUFFALO—LANCASTER (U.K.)
2022

Guernica Editions Founder: Antonio D'Alfonso

Michael Mirolla, editor
Interior design: Jill Ronsley, suneditwrite.com
Cover design: Allen Jomoc Jr.

Guernica Editions Inc.
287 Templemead Drive, Hamilton (ON), Canada L8W 2W4
2250 Military Road, Tonawanda, N.Y. 14150-6000 U.S.A.
www.guernicaeditions.com

Distributors:
Independent Publishers Group (IPG)
600 North Pulaski Road, Chicago IL 60624
University of Toronto Press Distribution (UTP)
5201 Dufferin Street, Toronto (ON), Canada M3H 5T8
Gazelle Book Services, White Cross Mills
High Town, Lancaster LA1 4XS U.K.

First edition.
Printed in Canada.

Legal Deposit—Third Quarter
Library of Congress Catalog Card Number: 2022934028
Library and Archives Canada Cataloguing in Publication
Title: Southwest of Italy : stanzas for a travel memoir / Federico Pacchioni.
Names: Pacchioni, Federico, 1978- author.
Series: Guernica world editions ; 55.
Description: 1st edition. | Series statement: Guernica world editions ; 55
Identifiers: Canadiana (print) 20220189706 | Canadiana (ebook)
20220189773 | ISBN 9781771837644 (softcover) | ISBN 9781771837651
(EPUB)
Subjects: LCGFT: Essays. | LCGFT: Poetry. | LCGFT: Travel writing.
Classification: LCC PR9120.9.P33 S68 2022 | DDC 828/.9208—dc23

To my mother, Carlina.

FOREWORD

FEDERICO PACCHIONI'S RICHLY REWARDING geographical memoir *Southwest of Italy* reminds me, in profoundly personal yet accessible ways, of the deep value of things only very partially under our control—history, place, emotion, coincidence, communities of friendship and affiliation, the trajectory of our times and the layers of meaning that make us who we are. I did not realize until now the list was so long.

Southwest of Italy undertakes to narrate its author's travels from his home, the "ancient nest" of Italy to the island of Sardinia, significantly off the southwestern coast of the Italian peninsula, and later his relocation further southwestward to the United States— first to Texas, then Arizona, and finally to Los Angeles—meeting along the way his wife and starting a family. "The journey southwest," Pacchioni writes, "has always been the defining one for me," and in his telling of it, this is far more than an individual coordinate or relative movement. The southwest, after all, is somehow "the southwest of the world," and heading in that direction here is following the arc of a life thoughtfully lived in environments carefully observed.

Part One describes Pacchioni's many trips to Sardinia and the clear affinity he feels for this "wild and archaic land," a place he associates with a kind of freedom that might be liberating, overwhelming, or confining. Sardinia is built on a "layering of cultures," as embodied in its legends and their relationship to the island's megalithic ruins, the Sardinian *Nuraghe,* as well as the island's history of conquest and colonization.

Part Two describes Pacchioni's move to the American south-west, where he begins the "unending negotiation between the modern promise of America and the old deep roots of Italy." Pacchioni describes the "desperate need for beauty," in these new southwestern spaces. Here too, he finds a layering of cultures, contemporary "folkloric" capitalism with the underlying model of prehistoric Puebloan lifeways.

The marks of our human past—whether in the ruins of Nuragic culture in Sardinia or the ruins of Puebloan culture at Palatki in Arizona—landscape historian John Brinckerhoff Jackson has argued, should be "signs of our sense of responsibility for the survival of the earth and its people."

I agree with Pacchioni that, in its spatial movement and its catalog of natural and cultural places and monumental geographies, *Southwest of Italy* has an unmistakable affinity for the genre of the travel narrative, particularly with what Paul Fussell calls its "conventions of self-consciousness and inward scrutinizing," and perhaps there is plenty of room for Pacchioni in a genre so expansive as to include Herodotus, Mark Twain, and Eric Newby. Pacchioni acknowledging that as a young man he kept a picture of Jack Kerouac on his wall and "juxtaposed" Kerouac against the imagery of Sardinia suggests that he feels at home in this company, and his references to D.H. Lawrence's 1921 *Sea and Sardinia* and Charles Fletcher Lummis's 1892 *Some Strange Corners of our Country* may underscore this.

For my part and because of my own geographical gestalt growing from a lifetime living in and writing about the American southwest, I tend to see Part Two of *Southwest of Italy* in the context of such excursionary and impressionistic narratives not only as Lummis's *Some Strange Corners*, but also John Van Dyke's *The Desert*, Mary Austin's *The Land of Journey's Ending*, J.B. Priestley and Jacquetta Hawkes' *Journey Down a Rainbow*, and even—for that matter—Jean Baudrillard's *America*.

But something here nags me beyond the taxonomy of travel writing. *Southwest of Italy* manifests a striking tension between the external and internal that may transcend Fussell's conventions. While deep with evocative descriptions of landscapes and locales, Pacchioni's memoir layers these external environments with a conceptual aesthetics, a dynamic apprehension of the world turning inward, as if exploring the caverns of Su Mannau in Sardinia or the "invisible underworld" of the mines beneath the Arizona boom town of Jerome, places perhaps both suggesting the "unexplored chambers of the self," the "metamorphosis inside." Language here works diligently to wrap around this ineffability, as water wraps around the body of a diver entering the sea, enveloping but not penetrating.

Pacchioni observes that *southwest* is "at once place and direction," so, of course, there are a few things we must discuss. Wallace Stegner, whose germinal essay "The Sense of Place" defines in many ways one of the trenches dug between modernist and postmodernist views of the American southwest, famously writes that "no place is a place until things that have happened in it are remembered in history, ballads, yarns, legends, or monuments." This notion of place clearly manifests itself in *Southwest of Italy*, where we are "elevated by ... fable."

On the other hand, as a direction or a trajectory, Pacchioni's southwest suggests something of what Stegner somewhat woodenly calls "migratoriness," a nomadic restlessness antithetical to a sense of place, but one that has become inescapable in a pan-regional and globalized view of where we are. *Southwest of Italy* probably engages with what David Simpson has described as a contemporary "discourse of situatedness," a kind of spatio-explanatory rhetoric that frames identity as a recounting of where we're coming from and where we're going.

I know, I know—I have casually and for lazy convenience simply been calling *Southwest of Italy* a *memoir*, but of course that may be accurate in only a crude synecdochical way. This is instead, we are told, a collection of *stanzas for* a memoir, one of the best subtitles I have read in a long time. Within our day-to-day notion of the basic metrical unit in a poem lives the Italian *stanza*, a standing, stopping place, a stationary moment placed within the moving timeline of memoir.

Southwest of Italy is a surprising synthetic project, fundamentally ecological, arguably dialectical in its sense of integration, its intuitive sense of experiential holism. I am afraid that for many of us perhaps, the so-called "spaghetti westerns" of Sergio Leone, some location shots for which were filmed in Sardinia during the 1960s and 1970s, have been the only midway points between Sardinia and L.A. Pacchioni tells us so much more.

Pacchioni ends *Southwest of Italy* on the road. I happily picture my friend and collaborator Federico and his family, mobile and trajectory-bound again after the pandemic lockdown, driving cross country at night "with stories to unwrap like snacks for the trip." We often associate storytelling with the short days and long evenings of winter when we gather closer together—around a fire, at a table, in a car even. At sunset on the winter solstice, the sun drops below the horizon farther to the southwest than at any other time.

For Federico, this direction is cardinal, and because the best memoirs, of course, never belong to their authors alone, so this compass point is now ours as well.

Reuben Ellis[1]

---

1   Dr. Reuben Ellis is author of volumes of criticism on Western American and Native American Literature such as *Vertical Margins: Mountaineering and the Landscapes of Neo-Imperialism*; *Stories and Stone: Writing the Ancestral Pueblo Homeland*; *Beyond Borders: The Selected Essays of Mary Austin*, as well as several works of fiction, poetry, and creative non-fiction.

PART ONE

I T HAS FINALLY HAPPENED. The Southwest has claimed me, permanently. It has kept its promise. It saved me from a frozen New England dead end. It provided a green oasis in the desert to channel my vein of desire, poetry's source, into a field of labor. And now that I'm its, I return to the pages of the book of my life, to the time I was reborn on this silent plateau, where I landed upon my first flight out of the ancient nest of Italy, in yet another move to the southwest of the world.

Any traveling eastward, be it to the midwestern gray trees of Indiana or the masonry harbors of Connecticut, always felt no more than that, traveling. No matter how lengthy, it came as an interruption of my true pilgrimage southwest, a pause in the music, sometimes so long-drawn to make me forget and doubt of my belonging here.

Now that the roots are clearly taking hold of the dusty and hard terrain, fracturing as they dig headfirst, reviving as they drink feverishly of the brilliant sap of illusions that this earth is known for, I can begin to understand what this desert has done to me these last twenty years, for half of my life, the American half.

Don't take me wrong. It has not been lonely, nor by any means a unique discovery. On the contrary, I have met many others like me, from previous and contemporary times, ensnared by the western dream, elevated by its fable, even exactly like me, from other similar walled-in nests, and I've searched their grounds for clues, as parallel realities of the self with differing faces and names.

There are other journeys that I might write about one day. Like traveling straight south, down along the Adriatic coast by a nostalgic pulsation of the heart, a gracefully funereal quest for communities that are no longer and blood forsaken by veins. Or like moving towards the center, which meant down across the Apennines and the plains of Lazio, to the stones of Rome—which regardless the direction of approaching, it's always a moment towards the center of all things, strangely always a movement slightly upwards, onto a dazzling arena of despotic causality, always more astonishing and disheartening than I imagined.

But the journey southwest has always been the defining one for me, the journeys of life-changing decisions, of overhauling the self, of unveiling reality. This has been so from the time the island of Sardinia started entering my mind, unconsciously etching there its barren and magical pictograph, calling me to the inevitable journey somewhere southwest of my nest. Then it was Texas, then it was Arizona, then it was Southern California, and the thaumaturgical rope might even pull me farther, in a spiraling attempt to grab the slippery ball of the planet, gradually retracing its circumference but never though stepping on the same grounds. My own dance around Earth.

I T ALWAYS STARTED WITH a crossing of the sea. And first, it was the stepping on a ferry reeking of restlessness, salt, and old pastries. I took that boat many times, and on each of them, I met with the same breed of ghosts. The liner left from the city of Civitavecchia. After passing through frumpish streets underneath buildings darkened by inches of condensed smog, I reached the purgatory of the embarkation zone. At last, the white and blue liners for Olbia, once Terranova, ingested my mind and body for about one day and one night.

It's the same route that D.H. Lawrence, another devotee of the southwest of the world, traveled, returning from his nine-day trip from Cagliari to Nuoro through the interior of the island, and then to Terranova along the coast, in January of 1921. As it seems from his *Sea and Sardinia*, he searched for the authentic roots of the European civilization. The attraction of most of Sardinia's visitors, in one sense or another, is to its image of wild and archaic land, as always, part truth and part instrumental representation. I have to admit that I too found there what I wanted to see.

In my teens, when I made my first trips to the island, the prospect of adulthood laid before me worried me. I sensed that the wrong decision would have caused losing my freedom, my openness, and eventually my trust in life. It was the universal voice of youth, that vitality that possesses us so utterly in those years, the power that allows us to feel everything is possible, but that we know deep down is only temporary. I saw in Sardinia a place where I could have preserved my freedom. I fantasized about becoming a shepherd or a farmer, perhaps like the silent, bizarre, and sorrowful

15

man whom I met through a common friend near Costa Rei, living in a tiny house painted with generous and bright coats of color, furnished with hand-made beds and tables I visited during my first stay on the island. He had bought a small piece of land at the foot of a green mountain and undertaken a life of farming and contemplation together with his wife and two sons. But, as it often happens in these cases, after a few years of bucolic living, the wife left, wanting the opportunities of civilization for her children. He had chosen to remain.

Like for that solitary father, I too saw in Sardinia a place where I could be overwhelmed by life. Onboard the Civitavecchia-Olbia liner, I floated almost every year suspended into the searing wide world of summer vacations, anxious to be stung deeply by the spiraling wasp of freedom. About ten years after Lawrence, Elio Vittorini crossed the same sea toward Terranova and his experience of the island. His recollections, *Sardinia as Childhood*, resonated with similar rejoicing at openness, at foreignness, and even at the mixture of sadness and happiness they present.

On every one of the occasions I spent crossing that band of sea, I recall the suspension of limbo but also an all-pervasive vein of excitement. Each passenger seemed to be doing something different with their elation. Some would eat candy bars or read until succumbing to drowsiness. Others would let their eyes go red in front of the TVs of the café. Others, who could not sleep on the itchy, barely reclining armchairs in the noisy hall, would wander around the waiting rooms, corridors and decks without aim. Among these passengers, I smelled the traces of poetry and wandered searching for a recess where I could be away from wind and humidity. There I stood watching and listening as if for an unnamed prey tunneling through brine, sheer darkness of sky, frightening darkness of sea, moving upon the roar of the balustrades and through silent travelers. I crept silently through the body of the ferry to catch it with the traps of words.

I recall the vision of a sailor standing in the gray night, against the upper smokestack. I stared at him without being noticed. The man looked just like Jack Kerouac in a picture I had on my bedroom wall. As the sailor stared away from me at the waters, I fantasized about Kerouac being still alive and working in secrecy for some Italian marine line company, forgotten in the dusty collective imaginary, sailing away between the islands of the Mediterranean. This ferry could have been a productive spot for him and the other American beat poets that I read avidly in those years, a sort of floating anthropological study for his modern Buddhist mind. And I dreamed of Kerouac's profile, juxtaposed against the white of these liner ships, with a fixed look into the eternal flooding drama, hands in his pocket as if stuck in a fleeting haiku long exposed to winds.

While under the hull, in the recesses of the boat, I let my mind fade away carried by buckets of nothingness; the sea frizzled, scribbling little phrases in the air until my thoughts would pick up on them and flow as the white ethereal foamy stair of the boat's wake or as its relentless low wings. That crossing, like a death, took me away, alone, and gave me over to the spell of night waves where I could see it all—what I had lived and what I would live. Sometimes I cried, sometimes I laughed until my heart was so full that I stormed back into the orange corridors wanting to tell somebody how excruciatingly beautifully life was blowing by. But it was late at night, and between the shadows of the salty wooden corridors, in the underworld of the waiting rooms, between the monotonous TVs and the pale couches and the stone-age video games, there was no one else but a few gray phantoms of nausea who had little reason in the world to care about the delicate alchemy of the boat's stride.

At any time during the crossing, Sardinia, the southwest, as a vague dream, was already there on that boat. And maybe when crossing on their way back, the islanders are for a moment led to doubt of their island's existence, and of themselves, fruits of a dream.

Finally, when the day started stretching his morning bones, and the night seemed gone as a sweet sonata, everyone fumbled around, and excited readied to debark. The boat's intricate metallic stomach system entered the crucial phases of its digestion: choking exhaust, cars sliding off unpredictably, bewildering screams, narrow staircases and maps of the boat's vivisections to decipher disparately. And when the prow kissed the seaport, implacably the limbo of the ferry started to fade like snow in the sun, and by the time foot or wheel touches the rough cement of the pier, all of it is vaporized and forgotten.

SOUTHWEST, AT ONCE PLACE and direction, is a bright cloud that never dissipates, not even against the bluest of skies; it is pervading and blinding. It's a strange nebula that one may fixate upon but not follow with the eyes; it descends and envelops our life from all sides and, to better claim us, it may even take human form.

For example, in my case, it changed into the figure of an alien goddess, stepping suddenly on the path. Her name Julie Ann, a pure embodiment of the intangible, stunning in her melancholic unworldliness. She condensed inside her a multiplicity of southwestern dream patterns across generations: her 20th-century parents', German war refugees now existing in the wreck of a Texan new beginning; her workplace's, a utopian food emporium chain that eventually drowned ideals in privilege; and of course, her own, a crusade to tame the mystery of creative inspiration. Blinding thick heavenly fog. In the alternative-seeking prism of the end of the millennium, Julie Ann's credo perfectly interlocked with my own equally powerful dream factories: my mother's Catholic activism, my father's fanatical devotion to a pristine principle of Art, Buddhism via American counterculture, a uniquely Romagnol anarchic Zen concocted by a cohort of eccentric guru friends, Mahatma Gandhi's memoir, enthusiastic revolutionary plans for a new poetry-ridden wholistic pedagogy, and probably more.

Julie Ann, faerie of the Southwest, immediately turned spouse, led me to see San Luca, and the green feet of the Apennines become smaller and smaller, from the window of that first airplane. After a year of Texas, we would be drawn to the western deserts, and, after many parentheses of time, settle in the fertile madness of Southern California, always propelled by the quest for the closest resemblance to our dreams. But that was the final point of the trajectory, starting from the geographical coordinates of Romagna, Italy, and tracing a route across half of the world.

Along that line lies the island of Sardinia, which I was thus to revisit again, after several other trips with friends or alone, in the company of Julie Ann, the destination for a honeymoon set strangely before the wedding, like an initiation or test for the veracity of our bond.

Sardinia, the harbinger of our southwestern destiny, fills many pages of the book of my memories, with fragments from that memorable preposed honeymoon, often retracing previous solitary routes.

I recall returning together to Stintino, where the sea carries a glittering that plays with the golden shores of the islands, as if a gigantic flock of marbles navigate underneath. Upon first sight of it, any resistance to the water's call melts away and one swims as if for the first time. The marbles of light roll through a strait between three smaller islets: Asinara the larger, Piana the mid-size, and Pelosa the smaller. Stringing together these islands one is left with a mournful amulet, encased with the fear and struggle against the threatening other, the destabilizing invader from without or within. The tiny speck of Pelosa is covered by an ancient defensive watch tower guarding for signs of the rising pirate epidemic, a sickness that scourged the costal communities of southern Italy for centuries; the larger Asinara was first a site of quarantine for those stricken by malaria, the invisible invader, and then at the end of the last century, it became a jail to isolate leaders of terrorist groups during the Years of Lead, and Mafia and Camorra bosses of the likes of Totò Riina and Raffaele Cutolo. The sense of menace and isolation emanating by this coast contrasts with the sea's crystalline colors and purity, twisting the heart with a strange sense of harrowing enjoyment and melancholia. Today many tourists bathe in this beautiful sadness, mindlessly perhaps, but immersed in it nonetheless.

OFTEN WE DON'T KNOW that we are dreaming, even when our illusions are our very motives, even when they might become the foundation of history itself. One has to pay attention to the details.

Driving through the complex wilderness of the Fluminese region of the island, we eyed a small sign for a historical site on the side of the road, an unknown place called Tempio di Antas, and, as it so often happens when driving through Italy, debated a few kilometers and, when curiosity finally won, turned back to take a cracked road disappearing into dark vegetation.

When the small road finally ended, we parked in an opening and walked on an uphill stony path. We reached the top and we saw, in the forceful sun, the temple. Wan slender columns amidst the imposing presence of overly-thriving vegetation appeared as the frail whitish legs of an elderly person lost in a pulsating impatient crowd of youth. The temple gave me a sense of misplacement and defenselessness. The stone sitting in the sun seemed to be emanating an acrid aroma. We walked through what appeared to once have been the main entrance and wandered around looking for signs left by ancient minds. An inscription on the pediment, "Sardus-Pater Babai."

Later, I would learn that Roman hands had built it upon a pre-existent Punic temple dedicated to the god Sid Addir Babai, after a struggle of two centuries to take the island, thus incorporating and translating local ancient cults. In turn, the inscription on the pediment embraces and reveals another layering of culture, this time by the natives who believed in the mythical figure of an ancient hero and father of the islanders, Sardus Pater. Roman histo-riographers of the time even researched the character and believed he had come from Libya with a valiant army to take the island eventually changing its name from Ichnusa to Sardinia. The temple is an example of the Romans' colonizing cunningness, at once em-bracing and redirecting a Punic god and a local patriotic figure into their new structure.

The temple, removed from the main road, hidden among thick trees, marked by a faint road sign, is actually the doorway to under-standing one of the secrets of the ancient empire's success, if not the universal malleability of human religions and cultures. We had almost missed it.

MAYBE, AS LEGENDS GO, the ancient Sardus Pater was the foreign sailor found on the white beach of Chia by Nora, the beautiful daughter of a king, having survived a shipwreck. Her people fed him and gave him a place to live, and he learned their language and became a good shepherd. One day, the thieves of the sea attacked the village. The newcomer proved himself to be also a good warrior, and with his strength and skills forced the pirates to retreat. After that, he was married to the princess and proclaimed Norax, the defender of Nora. The legend says that he then guided the other shepherds in building a new village, this time with huge impregnable stones, cut out of the nearby mountains, and arranged in conical shapes. The sea thieves could no longer ravage their homes. It's said that every shepherd learned from him the new building technique and, with the time, all of the islands' hilltops were lit up at night by stony dwellings.

This tale explains the many thousands of megalithic ruins, cone-like and cave-like structures of large stones called *Nuraghe*, which are identified with Sardinia. Today, along many roads, you can spot the ruins, half-hidden by olive trees flooded with sheep starving for shade, as large pieces of black bread surrounded by white ants.

SIX MILES NORTH FROM the temple of Antas, more ancient carving of stone has taken place, not the work of human hands but the river's, as it ate through the mountain to form the hollows of Su Mannau. As the name immediately implies to the Romance language speaker, these caverns are the domain of things fearsome. Indeed, since time immemorial, the natives have been known to enter the top levels, and leave offerings near sweaty stalagmites and unworldly pools, to parley with their nightmares.

Julie Ann and I imagined the gazes of the ancient folk, mixed with fear and attraction. Without the aid of modern light illuminating the path, this crevice represented a descent into a world of obscurity, lit only by torches. They had little idea of how long the system of caves was and where it led; the whole subterranean universe populated by mysterious creatures may very well have extended down forever. As they crept along those cold, wet, and rounded rocks in pitch dark, every sound and echo would have turned within their minds into the steps of monstrous and fierce creatures. The dense and silent heart of these verdant mountains was filled with holy terror, crowded with the human's eternal fascination and repulsion for the unexplored chambers of the self.

M Y GUTS IN KNOTS, I postpone at the edge of rocks, above that undulating stranger, consensus of waves, until, ready, I dive. And when inside, I look up and see the delicate crystalline placenta and sun tears. I push back with all my fins as a newly-born fish—I see. I am wrapped by the finest silk of constant freshness, and a beautifully mottled liquid sky kisses my trembling flesh. I play in shallow water with schools of fish, trying to be accepted into their uniform society—I don't turn quickly enough and I am spurned.

Looking in the underwater distance, from inside, something frightens me: darkness of blues, misty sparkles of mesmerizing oblivion. I go farther if I can proceed with a friend, keeping sight of his familiar features. Crossing the branches of a small gulf, I fly over grassland of gray tubular seaweeds, flowing forward and backward, my intention almost useless. Underneath a dusky watchtower, confronted by stairs of stones closing into an untrustworthy green-black well, my heart explodes. I wallow back to the shore with disquietude in my legs.

THE PITILESS SUN OF the island's interior made every piece of the car scalding to the skin. A bottle rolled back and forth underneath the seat. Where does the sea go when you travel inland? If the region Julie Ann and I were traveling through, Barbagia, is really the heart of Sardinia, as many say, the sea, as blood, should run here along its vital paths. I sought to glimpse around me that brilliance, that smell, and that subtle rhythm sea-waters have. I sought to detect the sea through the small jumps of the divining rod of the heart, probing subtle turns of the wind, a spark in the air, or calmness throughout the streets of mountain towns. I would find it there, a dirt road near the town of Orune, following a little sign indicating a site called Su Tempiesu.

We parked at the edge of a cliff and started walking on a path stretching through thick brush along a mountainside that descended into valleys of moorland far in the distance, yellow and green. We proceeded on the trail that soon entered into a thick vegetation. Down the path, in front of us, we heard voices. We came to a clearing, where two men were working at the site removing fallen branches and weeds. We stepped into the open area exchanging greetings and saw, almost hidden by the land side, a vertical structure enclosed by a sharp triangular roof. It was quite small and of an aesthetics foreign to me. At first sight, it gave me the impression of being the grotesque house of some goblin. The two men seemed happily surprised upon seeing us there and began explaining that what we were standing next to was a construction by the Nuragic culture of the later part of the second millennium BCE, made at the apex of their splendor. They pointed to the inside of the structure, where a trickling sound of water came from a small circular room. In brief, we came to know that this was a temple dedicated to water—quite sacred to the ancient people. In Nuragic times it seems that only the priests could approach the water collecting in the inner room, while the faithful could gather around outside the structure. Due to the findings of many small votive sculptures in bronze all around the vicinity, it was concluded that people were brought here for healing, and maybe to consecrate important decisions.

In spite of the ancient priests, we sat right on the small steps and let the cold soft water run through our fingers. This was the first natural spring we had seen in quite a while. The sound of that trickling rivulet, underneath that cool tympanum shelter, and its liquid string running clear through the channel of rocks, seemed to penetrate deeply into my bones, quenching my very cells. In this inland, the soul of the sea laid prostrated, submissively proffering its secret powers.

S TANDING AT THE EDGE of the coast, especially at sunset, filled me with a sense of great solitude. Yes, the island is isolated, not only the land but also everything that feeds on it and that touches it. Every plant and animal, every man and house seemed to have been left alone to itself in some warehouse of the universe.

I have memories of Sardinian beaches as shores of the cosmos, as edges where you can forget to exist and just sit for long days sipping reality as through the straw of an indescribable cocktail. Lying down on the fresh fine sand in the shade of contorted trees, I was once caught by the transient fingers of life. In a twilight state, I was dragged into a dream of the debris of the world—chewed, spit, and kicked by the elements of the universe. Dried tangled seaweed, ants dispersed by gusts of wind, dramatically polished barks, sun and shade, and I, hypnotized, underneath trees reduced to kneeling by an ancient wind, and all a background to the roaring emblematic symphony of transition—the sea, weary thick sea.

Or standing on rocks turning pink in the sunset, I assisted the rippling dark blue sea by making ballads out of my life. Kidnapped by the vision of a living horizon, whispering and rising between the frames of prehistoric irregular granites, I forgot my name. And for hours, the thought of the pure ice-cold set within submarine valleys, sunk through my bones and wobbled up the stairs of my DNA, crystallizing my attention into the patience of some immortal creature.

These sensations came back to me again when I heard the soft and perky echoing sound of the Tenores di Bitti, one among the many traditional polyphonic music groups of Sardinia. Four singers form these groups, accompanying Sardinian traditional celebrations. With their round harmony, they serve a vast span of purposes: inviting dance, embodying nostalgia, reflecting on worldly matters, praying, amusing, and teaching. Their half-sung, half-spoken chant takes over the mind very much as the Sardinian sea does, placing every thought and emotion within a larger context.

A tenores chant can contextualize and heal even the most bitter side of existence. In the Taviani brothers' film *Padre padrone*, the shepherd father, having realized he had punished his son too severely, takes the child in his arms and begins to sing a melody. Suddenly, other shepherds from nearby posts, and the whole Sardinia in a sense, join the father's chant giving to his cry a larger place in the scheme of life's harshness, in the struggle for survival, a way for him to exist in his violence.

At the Nuragic village and sanctuary of Santa Cristina, I saw a sacred Nuragic well that recalls the structure of Su Tempiesu but upside-down, a reversed triangle, illustrating this time the feminine principle. It goes underground instead of upward. A stair descends into a cave in a truncated pyramid shape. I walked down together with a small party; the guide was pleased to hear I had visited the well in Orune. At the end of the stairway was again a circular room where water runs all year round. As I was looking from the inside toward the exit, the blazing sun of the day made the opening into a blinding perfect trapezoid. Here, too, the well had been a temple.

Years later, far from there, along my trajectory southwest, I stood by Montezuma's Well, in Arizona. The two places connect across time and space. Montezuma's Well is a large sinkhole caused by the collapse of an underground cavern that filled with water and is still running today. Since there are very few oases in the area, the beneficial influence of the liquid is felt whenever the well is approached. It is a sacred place for the Yavapai Indian tribe, who view this site as a natural *sipapu*, the entrance through which all living creatures made their first appearance in the world. In these two desert lands, so strangely similar in many ways, I've learned how water has been a sacred element, a medium for ceremony. The liquid master makes living creatures round with his babbling limpidly, smoothes the edges of the body, and not only of that, swallowing all confusion. At night, I was assailed by dreams of Oceans vast, mythical, and blue as I never dreamed of before.

THE CAR CLIMBED UP a rugged steep hill ablaze in the light. On its top, at the end of the road, I saw a curious wall of white, pink, and brown houses. In the midst of that brownish irregular landscape, they seemed excessively bright and geometrical. Suddenly the dwellings reminded me of the piles of construction toys I used to scatter at home, irritating my mother's sense of order. Orune is a place that mesmerized me for its otherness compared to what I knew of Italy. I had the impression to have found some secret ganglion of the Sardinians' mystery. The Barbagia region, protected by the arms of the massif of the Gennargentu, had been a refuge for the islanders against the Carthaginians, the Romans, and the other invaders.

Many of the historical and cultural traces one finds here speak, directly or indirectly, of what Sardinia as a whole has undergone through history, caught in an ever-changing political redefinition coming from the outside, seeking a core shelter from preying seafarers and colonizers.

When walking through the streets of Orune's neighboring town, Orgosolo, famous for its history of uneasiness and rebellion against the State, one realizes how much modern Sardinian identity has shaped itself around a repurposing of these ancient dynamics seeking to become a global emblem for liberation against oppression. The walls of Orgosolo are covered with murals from the hands of anarchic and university groups that associate the story of these people with a myriad of other stories of resistance throughout the world. Strolling through the town, one passes from the images of daily Sardinian life to the memorials of struggles among bandits and carabineers, and then to those against fascism and NATO. Side by side to images of popular bandits are portraits of Gramsci and an American tribal chief.

The idea of the bandit as champion of Sardinian independence and freedom, however, has been much romanticized, encompassing so many different symbols, from that of regional independence and resilience against external and centralizing powers, the northern-centered Italian State first and foremost, to the projection of a post-industrial urbane culture seeking a sense of the primitive wild and disenfranchisement from modern capitalism. In reality, of course, the acts of the so-called bandit have been, certainly since the second half of the last century, shameful crimes, such as kidnapping, stealing, and murdering, more often than not motivated by the mere quest for quick and easy gains.

It is true that Sardinians, as in the case of Sicilians and many colonized cultures around the globe have been long uneasy and in conflict with State's laws. Mainly because of the political instability resulting from the continuous substitutions of one dominator for another, Sardinians have found themselves having to face anarchy. It is in such circumstances that societies often give rise to local forms of justice passed on through custom rather than constitutions, without the need of third-party legitimation and mediation, as it happened on this island, probably since ancient times, to maintain some kind of order within and between the communities. The fabled Codice Barbiricino, the code of Barbagia, does hold some truth, perhaps even still today, in the manner in which a silent understanding exists among the people. One of the characteristics of this code is the "culture of revenge" or *balentia*.

Balente is a man of honor and a virile individual who is fighting for his reputation, defending the social status of his family and of his community. Violence has played a crucial role in Sardinian society. Through it, physical strength, as well as mental cunningness, can be easily proven to the community. This sense of honor partially regulates the ways through which offenses against oneself or one's family have to be avenged in order to confirm or reaffirm the status of men, women, and clans. The revenge is planned carefully in order to stand as a clear and proportionate response to a received wrong. The offenses range from insult to damage and theft of propriety or animal, to trickery, and to harm of the person. The more an offense leads to permanent damage, the more serious it is considered. But the criteria for the evaluation of an offense are not all objective, and subjectivity leads to conflicting interpretations concerning the kind and the seriousness of the vengeance required to bring "justice." Therefore, since the two opposed parties often have divergent views on this matter, the common result of "the culture of revenge" is a long-drawn family feud, one of the many so-called *disamistade* that poisoned the air of many Sardinian towns.

"Disamistade," which could be translated as hostility, appears as the title of one the songs of the last record of the folk singer Fabrizio De André, *Anime Salve*. The song intensely expresses the emotional roots and ramifications of being trapped in Sardinian feuds. De André lived most of his life in an ancient villa set in a remote location of the island. In 1979, he experienced the ordeal of being kidnapped and held captive, together with his wife, somewhere in the impervious areas of Supramonte. Perhaps, the album that was recorded right after his liberation, *Indiano*, was De André's attempt to understand as well as to educate others about the reality of the Sardinians. On the cover of this record stands a Cheyenne armed with a rifle, riding a horse through a bare landscape. In the lyrics, the peculiar juxtaposition between Sardinia and the American West goes beyond the purely choreographic, which has been after all one already testified by the many Spaghetti Western films shot on the island. *Indiano* explores the tribal non-Western characteristics of Sardinian mentality. While songs such as "Quello che non ho" (That Which I Don't Have) show the Sardinian free mindset in comparison to the consumerist dilemma of the modern continental, other songs such as "Canto del servo pastore" (Chant of the Shepherd Servant) let a premodern animism transpire through the lyrics.

Somehow the heartbeat of this island southwest of Italy, in all its silent tumultuousness, matched the rhythm of my own teenage heart, defiantly righteous, tenderly prickly, wildly spellbound. I had my brother paint a Sardinian landscape on my wooden guitar. I learned to play De André's songs. I carried the island's indrawn knot of verse and music to the hills of my beloved Apennines, casting its baleful charm on the night fire of my circle of friends.

YEARS BEFORE, IN THE company of friends, I was following the signs for Torre della Fava (Tower of the Fava Bean), the fanciless but luminous structure we had seen through the car's windows coming up the main road of Posada. A story says that when the Saracens invaded from the sea and besieged Posada for a long time, the town's people had fed a dove with the last fava bean and let it fly as a false courier from the main tower to some non-existing allied town. The Saracens spotted the bird, captured it, and finding the bean in its stomach, believed the people of Posada still had provisions and support to spare, and already fearful for malaria spreading through their ranks, left with all their fleet. Apparently, a bean can change the tides of history.

Getting to Posada's top was not an easy thing in the heat of the midday; a lukewarm wind blew over the battered alleys of the town. We reached the entrance to the tower wheezing and sweating. Inside, the only light besides the door was the ceiling hatch breached by a rustic ladder; we wobbled, blinded by the contrast between the absolute light we had been swimming through and the virgin moist obscurity of the room. We climbed carefully up the ladder, till we were again immersed in light. The summit of the tower was a square balcony fenced by a low metal balustrade. And the wind came rushing over us as on the deck of a ship amidst high sea. Except the ship was as large and heavy as the whole island itself. High up there, we could understand how the earth swarming with vegetation dove into the waters. On the other side, mountains wrinkled growing darker as far as we could see and their breath ravaged our hair as the exhale of an entire world. It seemed the incommensurable depth of this world was looking directly up at us, endowing a primordial trust, as if we had become, by stepping up there, the lookouts for the island's journey through time.

ALONE, ON THE HIGHWAY right out of Olbia, on a sunny day, I got a ride with two young men in a car crowded with climbing gear. Amazingly enough, they had been directed south to the town of Escalaplano that was not too far from San Vito, the town I was headed to. Rather than the coastal roads, they took the faster way through the interior. We passed lands that had been burned by the fires which often return there at the approaching of the summer, too often by the hand of men. After having driven up-hill quite a bit, we reached the town of Escalaplano where I was left on my own. I don't think that many strange-looking teenagers with jingling backpacks passed through the remote and bare Escalaplano. I walked across the stony narrow streets of the town. I suddenly felt as if I had stepped into a party where everyone knew each other but I knew no one and therefore my every movement turned awkward. I walked through a group of old men, all dressed in gray and black suits and hats. I sensed having been keenly observed even though they were eyeing me with discreet dissimulation. Escalaplano is a peak striking into the sky. The view underneath is ample and only with difficulty I could discern the forms of the yellow earth below. I thought of those men, living up there, almost outside Sardinia, as a Tibetan village above the clouds where guardians of humanity play their inscrutable schemes in incognito.

That day I had another ride with an old man in a tiny dusty car to the nearby town of Ballao. Along the way, he warned me of the dangers of hitchhiking in these remote places, but it didn't faze me; there was no turning back for me, by now a lamb over the altar of travel. I was left on the outskirts of Ballao, at the interchange to the street that led to San Vito. It was about 30 kilometers to the village, and, judging how expeditious things had been going all day, I had no doubt I would get another ride soon. After attempting for about an hour on the same spot, I decided to start walking to a better launching pad. The street was wider than I had expected and cars came running fast perhaps not even noticing my backpack that camouflaged against the hills nor my thumb sticking out in need. I walked about 15 kilometers that afternoon under a scorching sun. My beach shoes had thin soles that started to disappear; in a moment of desperation, I cut two large leaves from a prickly pear cactus, cleaned them thoroughly of thorns and attempted to tie them together with my shoes as new soles. But they did not stay, and I just gritted my teeth at the burning asphalt. Also, my two-gallon water supply was running short and the street signs told me there was still a long way to San Vito. I walked through black tunnels, as close as I could to the greasy walls to avoid the cars flying a few inches by me. On one side of the street, arid and rocky hills rose steep, and on the other, a precipice gave way to wide distances.

At dusk, when I had begun looking for a safe recess beyond the silvery curb where I could spend the night, a jeep stopped. The man driving seemed sorry at the sight of a young fellow like me walking in the middle of nowhere at nightfall. With enormous relief, I sunk into the soft front seat. When finally in San Vito, I ran directly toward the first *bar*, bought myself a cold beer, and sipped it as slowly as I could sitting at a table outside. In the fresh evening, I felt as the sunbaked survivor out of some Western caravan-wreck. That evening I walked to the house of a friend I had met during my first trip to the island. His family welcomed me and shared with me a dinner of fresh vegetables and meat. I was exhausted, and further celebration was postponed to the next day. That night I slept on the balcony-roof of the house, with the rest of the family, as is the custom during the hot summer nights. Many other houses had similar gray balcony-roofs, where surely other families fell asleep snoring on thin mattresses. I recall the day-warm cement underneath me soothing my sore back and legs and the stars that glimmered above us like above a camp of nomads.

IT WAS A FEW years before, I was staying in Villaputzu, on the South East coast, in the home of a friend's grandparents. One day the grandfather decided to show us a special hidden beach, tourist-free, in a locality called Quirra. He drove his tiny car with the utter absence of rush on uneven dirt roads. We came to a hilly area, and much to my surprise, I noticed strange rounded structures, bluish-greenish metallic bubbles, set on the very top of numerous hills. Puzzled, I asked my friend about them. The installations belonged to a nearby NATO military base.

The marine air entered more and more from the car's wide-open windows, while drops of sweat sparkled from underneath the old man's gray hat. He was a short stocky man in his seventies with vivid black eyes and an unpredictable mood, both of which I observed being common among the islanders. In the span of an hour, he could go from absolute silence to an explosion of humor. I still think of him often, pressing grapes in his garage, cleaning prickly pears, mixing cold sparkling water with wine at lunch.

My friend told me that, since the man's wife had fallen sick with cancer, he hadn't been the same. When we stepped out of the car, I was shocked by the sudden release of ferocity with which he enacted his revenge on a small green praying mantis that had dared to jump on the neck of his shirt, throwing it on the ground and giving it one precise and long-drawn stomp. He quickly returned serene and playful, excited to share the beautiful spot he had known since his childhood and pleased to make us happy with a day by the sea. Almost unconsciously he blocked the bluish-greenish metallic bubbles from his gaze.

We were struck by the beauty of the site, yet my friend looked melancholic; under her smile was bitter irony. At the time I did not know of the full scale of suffering caused by military test sites such as the one in Quirra, nor their shameful and impenetrable secrecy. Though I remember a growing eeriness haunting me the day as my young mind started connecting the dots: the iron domes, the grandmother, the mantis. I swam in the deceivingly crystalline waters and played my guitar on the granite boulders trying to chant myself away; they did not sing back.

THE ICON OF THE American tribal chief had appeared to me another time—tattooed on the arm of a young man, on a warm evening on a beach near Muravera, during that first stay on the island. I had come to know a group of young people in the nearby town of San Vito. Among these, there was a tattoo artist who, with his homemade needle-pen, carved the spiral I have on my chest. The American Indian face was also his creation. The night I received my tattoo, he had prepared both of us with a bottle of Mirto, which I had never tasted before. The cool of the night and the chilled liquor completely cleansed from me the heat of the day. The intent was to anesthetize me and provide inspiration to him. I recall walking with a festive group of young men and women toward a pewter part of town populated with what seemed to be miniature houses of cement.

During my stays, I have collected memories of young Sardinians gathering on small, moon-pale streets, or against the thick walls protecting old towns from the unpredictable sea, joking and laughing loudly in their Sardinian accent and words, held by the feverish hands of Mirto. But also, I recall in their dark eyes a look of dense melancholy and uneasiness spreading. Melancholy for the world beyond that sea perhaps, the world they stared at through their small kitchen TVs. As if they had been weighed down by an unwanted responsibility toward a crippled and yet sacred land, an island that chained their lives and yet gave them a solid and respectful sense of identity. I could not mistake the way I was often looked at and envied for the possibilities I had as a young man living in the continent.

Perhaps every young Sardinian is faced in their life with the choice to become fully Sardinian or not. Staying is compared to marrying the island for better and for worse, in good times and bad times, and therefore accepting a challenging cultural responsibility and running the risk of fossilizing underneath the mask of ancestors. I imagine that this feels a little like boarding a ship already on its way to sinking or like being baptized to an irremediably disenchanted religion. In the family I observed, I seemed to glimpse the anxiety and conflict that the demand of such a decision creates. I couldn't help but notice in the parents who, palpating an undercurrent of discontentment and drive to escape, will attempt to exorcise the problem by ignoring it or by developing in their children a sense of shame deriding anything not Sardinian. And here I find a reason for that American Indian tattoo since Native Americans are indeed faced with the same kind of problem as in Louis Owens' novel, *Dark River*, with those young natives who are torn apart by the question of whether to be traditional or not to be traditional. The situation of Sardinian youth reminds me of the diaspora that has shaped my own self and that of my fellow nationals, the unending negotiation between the modern promises of America and the old deep roots of Italy.

One evening, I saw, just before sunset, a young man taking his girlfriend between his arms and diving together into the sea—the curves of their bodies so shiny and full. They swam together and played in the ruby waves and then came back to the beach where he wrapped her affectionately into a large towel. What does it mean to be in love and to be born on the same island? I wondered, pitying and envying them at the same time.

The tattoo artist owned one of the minuscule cubicles of cement making up one of the sections of the town of San Vito. Since he had lost his key, he jumped, with dexterity, up to the roof to access what he termed "the back entrance." With a bandana around his head, his dark complexion and bright black eyes against the starry night, he looked like a pirate of some nineteen-century sea legend. Next, he appeared on the inside of the house, opening the small door, and inviting us to make ourselves comfortable. Inside, I tried playing the guitar I used to bring with me everywhere at that time. It was the same bruised classical guitar upon which my brother had painted green lands encountering blue waters—to me, the prehistoric coast of Sardinia. The colors of the oil paint on my guitar were vivid, and when I stared at them pinching the strings, they shone against my eyes. While playing, I stood hypnotized for hours, with ear pressing against the guitar as against the thin wall of a cathedral where a celestial choir reverberated.

But that night in San Vito, I was too anesthetized to play, and soon I found myself lying on a table. The tattoo artist started his surgery work on the bony center of my torso. I gave him one clue only—"spiral". He was free to bring this element out as his creativity best told him so. I wanted something spiraling that would consecrate me once and for all as a living heart relentlessly swallowing up, in a vortex, all that life has to give. Perhaps the spirit of Vittorini had suggested the tattoo during the Mirto-induced trance. I floated away on the table as on a magic carpet. I recall the concentrated expression of the tattoo artist over me for long hours, during which a tickling delicate drill made a background to my epic dreams. I woke up late morning, and next to the table, the artist was sleeping against his chair—my tattoo incomplete.

PART TWO

I T RAINED FOR SEVERAL days straight, the first month of Texas. Mosquitoes waiting with the patience of cats for window screens to open to enjoy a free meal. A pair of large blue jays were building their nest on the tree facing our bedroom, and in the morning, they sang loudly, waking us to our new reality, Julie Ann's and mine, together across the great sea.

The days went by calm. I stared at the densely shaded courtyard of our apartment complex in the North side of Dallas letting things settle—the water in the pool vibrating with each blow of wind, the twittering of unknown birds. At night, every spot of green emanated an intense sound, a type of amplified sitar, the cicadas, the birds of the Texan night, until we would forget about them, about everyone, and that electric wave would become a bright backdrop to all else. Memories besieged me like movies, especially before sleep, as soon as I lay down, beautiful memories of a different world. All of my past surfaced at night, like a dream, emerging as never before. A deep transformation was taking place in my mind.

THE FIRST TIME I saw many people together was on my first 4th of July, only a few weeks after my arrival in Texas. While I strolled through streets bulging with roots, I had the sensation of having landed upon the body of a sleeping giant, moving amidst a people of minuscule beings who had constructed there a civilization.

On shreds of grass, among parking lots, families chattered and read; children adorned with phosphorescent strips ran with bags of potato chips larger than themselves; others danced rap on the roofs of cars. Adults, equipped with folding chairs, held enormous cups of cold drinks—oh the American disposable straw cup! Everyone waited for the fireworks, which exploded along with shouts, howling and applause from the crowd. Large and bright fireworks to represent how well-off the city was. What a spectacle those lights against the skyscrapers at night! It was like being in front of some majestic empire of the past, so great and strong that I could hardly fathom it.

I had a picture of predecessors in mind, those first Italian immigrants watching similar explosions of light around the Statue of Liberty fifty or a hundred years before, with the same awe and enthusiasm for being part of such grand feast, where ideas could take flight and blossom as easily as those sparkling stars.

W HY DOES ONE FEEL nostalgia? Not much for places or people, but for their projections inside us. I didn't miss my Italy, my Romagna, but how Italy and Romagna made me feel. Basically, I missed a certain self, a certain Federico. It might be that we are only nostalgic about ourselves in the end.

But the mind is one thing and the heart is another, and the latter experiences all as truly present. And I sensed the love of my sister Ilaria, my brother Francesco, my mother and father, their concerns, their hopes. To them, in those early days in America, I wrote the most heartfelt letters of my life. The letters were unaware of what they contained. They became a way to introduce my arising new self to the old self, a way of lovingly sowing the two strands together.

For my evolving heart nothing was routine, and the smaller signs reaching me from across the Ocean started to acquire larger meaning, to speak of an entire people. A way of life, forged by another time and place, transpired from even the shape of a package, the angle of a pen, the tracing of a seemingly meaningless address. My mother's letters were strewn with tiny shells from the Mediterranean.

The day Julie Ann and I understood the full scale of our craving for a different environment, we drove to Oklahoma. Finally, I was able to savor the large spaces of this part of the world, the stark plain ever widening in the distance, with roads unfathomably long and straight going in every direction, built by equally unfathomable hands.

Close to the border, the world changed and everything became green and filled with woods. We stopped at a site dominated by a large waterfall and surrounded by boulders. The squirrels there, accustomed to travelers, were friendlier then those in our Dallas backyard. Along the river, where the water formed pools, people of many origins bathed: Japanese, Africans, Mexicans, Indians, Europeans ... and all of them seemed to find for a moment a childhood freedom, in the cool mountain water, away from the eternal conflict of the city. Julie Ann and I talked about urbanization, environment, and dreamed of some utopian balance, somewhere in the Southwest.

THE SUN TOOK OFF in the morning and shone slanted on the neighborhood, on the clean upgraded townhouses, on the passersby dragging their dogs on the sidewalk in their neurosis of time. The sacred grounds of Dallas' residential neighborhoods, where no noise can be made, no shops, no traffic, only peace, squirrels, birds and pools. Right outside this enclave, rivers of giant cars, flowing without end on the multi-lane street. For a brief interval of time, until about 9 a.m., it was cool out, and I strolled practicing my good morning phrases.

Even the dark and large crows enjoyed the tender light and chill and calmly pranced around in utter liberty, holding some great wisdom to themselves. Walking along the artificial stream, occasionally, I entered a part of the path that had turned slightly wild, where I could meet something more than human logic.

The summer sun painted almost all of the grass yellow, rose along its flaming path, burned everything, us included, who, in the evening, as pieces of hot charcoal eased ourselves down in the freshness of a pool. It was all a cycle of thermal excursion.

AGAIN WE TOOK THE straight and majestic road. This time towards Arkansas. It opened before us as a uniform structure of green. Simulating a courage seated somewhere deep in me, I was swallowed up by a type of prehistorical present, America's history, the planet's charm dancing me to the roots of my human body and mind. The north of Arkansas reminded me of the hills that melt the peaks of the Apennines into the Po Valley, only infinitely vaster and uncultivated, irremediably leveled under a sky carved by the gliding of eagles.

At night, we set camp sheltered inside forests of tall trees, in spritely reverence, like children amid an educated crowd of gentlemen. The darkness crowded with life like the most teeming of mornings.

At dawn, with woodpecker's hammering and new bird's parodies of sentences, the sun pulled the strings of our eyelids, which opened as those of marionettes at their debut.

Immersed in our harmony of origin, we became painters, poets, musicians. The city's caves, lined with mirrors, could not provide the nourishment the soul needs, wonder. None of us returned home empty handed.

JULIE ANN ASLEEP, I awake. Again the need to reflect, to account for the metamorphosis inside. I felt the necessity to remain close to my native language, undertaking an infinite work of translation, finding the balancing point between two worlds that are in the end one and identical. While shifting constantly, human-kind appeared to me remaining the same at its base, a boundless sea with a luminous, empty and perfect bottom.

In general, nowadays, Italians in America are curious beings, a kind of attraction, defined by a temptation of vanity, walking heads up, flaunting an elected origin, their urbane wisdom, connoisseurs of foods and history, somehow immune to the perils of modernity. But that is how America wants us, because we are America's alter ego, we represent what it doesn't have and may never have due to the trajectory it has chosen. It struck me how many Americans boasted about having been in Europe and itched to explain it to me. Especially the wealthy clients of the food emporium where Julie Ann and I worked during that first year in Dallas. It seemed that they had all returned from a trip to Italy. And it struck me how many asked me what in the world had led me to leave my earthly paradise for Texas. I answered in common places, convenient stock phrases, but the truth was that I had been swept up by events that seemed bigger than me, the ardor for Julie Ann and for the fateful path that she opened in front of me.

Some who spoke a little Italian jumped up vivaciously when discovering my origin and began a conversation only for the plea-sure of vocalizing Italian words. In the meantime, I sold them cheese and salami. I became a bit of a merchant rather quickly, and in that way, I found my place in the dominating capitalistic current. Capitalism felt like a current here, not something political as I had been instructed at home, it had a folkloric flavor, it was a shared quest for a mysterious holy grail, the elusive business, whatever it may be, moved not so much by a cold monetary calculation, but by the desire to enter the circle of the financially independent. I often heard repeated, as if it were an idea from the Bible summing up the entire existence: "You won't make real money until you'll have your own business." We are not free men until we don't have our own business, only then we are riding the economy, rather than being swept up by it. I met characters at various levels of the great game of business. Some were bitter specialists, knowers of the rules, who had chased business all of their lives, almost grasped it, but never completely. Others were riding the wave nimbly like snakes, driven by some mystic force. Others had given up on pursuing it and entered the long lines of the spectators applauding the winners from the side of the track. American economy showed itself to my eyes of newcomer as a great country fair, complex in its regulations yet permeated by the simple emotional nature and spontaneous passion of the participants.

These were the days I learned how to drive on the great American highways, moving in sync with schools of shiny cars streaming within the triangle of Dallas, Denton and Ft. Worth.

I STARTED SEEING ITALY FROM outside; actually, I started seeing it for the first time, becoming aware of its culture, seeing its borders, its palisades, its plots, and traps. It's like observing a landscape; I need to approach it from a wider point of view, from above, to comprehend its features and uniqueness, to appreciate how it made me feel when I lived inside it. However, when I grow tired of observing, when the height causes me to feel alone, and the mountain's wind numbs my bones, I realize how observation by itself cannot fill my life.

SOUTHWEST CALLED. WE HAD decided to drive to Arizona, each taking the wheel, driving to the end of Texas, towards Amarillo, and then through New Mexico towards the glorious Santa Fe, spend a few days moseying around the mysterious territories of low brownish pueblos, artists, visionaries, green chili … and then through the painted stone forest, the rocky desert, to the verdant peaks of Flagstaff. There we planned to set base for various expeditions: Arcosanti, the urban laboratory in the desert designed by an Italian seeking a new and harmonious way to experience modernity, the mystical Sedona, Indian reservations, archeological sites inside canyons, an intriguing school called Prescott College— looking for our ideal new home or land wherever it might be.

I remember the excitement that filled us the days before leaving. We had a desperate need for beauty, trees, mountains, sky, pure air, and human stories that we could inhabit. Trusting that we would find our port, those days were tinted with magic, like before a great new step, before being welcomed by something magnificent and profound.

A ROSARY OF PURE SENSATIONS is engraved in the book of my memories from that first dive in the deep Southwest.

Heading towards Wichita Falls. Being overtaken by the realization that the expanse is all that matters: when the land lifts you up, and the center of the mind opens wide, and vastness is felt even with closed eyes, and what you spot in the land becomes in-significant, a series of patches in an infinite tapestry against which your remains rest, and on the barren land you make out all that you know exists: tropical islands, white bears, icebergs, the Kremlin, the Chinese Wall ... the realization that nothing is more abundant than the desert, by the same token a white canvas is full to the brim.

Inside Palo Duro Canyon. Like an enormous cradle, widening blue sea depth dried up by an age of sun, where we descend to find a shelter that makes us its own and becomes the world.

Passed Las Cruces's military testing site. The land cleanly divided between plain, flat sweep in the distance, and mountain, enormous spurs like ribs of the planet. I felt a weariness in that place, as if the land was throwing its arms down, as if it had lowered its head.

Inside the Enchanted Circle. Around us an immense distance of plains and mountains sweetly unfolding an ocean of earth, which seems to have been laboring forever towards a spot at the center. This island is uncrossable without becoming its. A wise island arisen like a soft idea of the planet, an explosion of life that makes you cover your mouth with a hand. Inside every small thing is a sacred universe. The atmosphere is difficult to snatch because it's enveloping and seemingly smiling to every act or thought, and peo-ple are children or prey of this enchantment, with eyes in which you can lose yourself or from which you can flee in fear. Inside, lightly grasped, the secret palm of the rock, where you can be part of the choir of this immense temple forever.

Canyon Road Color. Sitting by the fire. Above us there is a deep sky. Stars are the windows of the house of God. Our hearts are to-. gether where the smoke is lost.

T HE JOURNEY HAD LASTED a thousand years. We returned with prodigious loot. We now saw the city with different eyes and knew that the solutions that we believed impossible did actually exist. The people we met, the ideas we discovered in the quarries of our own beings cast many hopes into our future, and hope is something we were determined to satisfy. Three things became clear.

I understood that culture is not opposed to nature, that there is no duality between the two, and that culture, through its development, separates from nature and then eventually returns closer to it. I finally saw culture and humanity immersed in an inevitable harmonizing process by which, willing or not, balance is eventually found through life or death.

I understood that my talents were the channels through which this balance must occur in my life, the coordinates where I and the world intersect more intensively and deeply, where truth can more easily pass. I saw how this work called for a balance between confidence and humility. Confidence being the celebration of that unique intersection, and humility being the awareness that what has worth comes from outside myself, from something much greater.

I understood that the desire for beauty is the sign of the living soul, a force towards growth. It might seem to torture us with irreparable dissatisfaction, but only when we experience it passively, as victims. I saw how this yearning shouldn't be cursed, but thrown to the roots of our days, stalked, undressed until its last seducing garment. It should not be imprisoned to scenarios relegated to a far-away time and space but encountered exactly where we are, and the gulf of life will open. We moved to Prescott, Arizona.

WAKING UP IN PRESCOTT, the paths I could choose from were many, the pines tall and aromatic. A few wooden houses peeked between the trees, and on the higher slopes, the national forest advanced. From the peak of the iconic rock called Thumb Butte, one could see the surrounding land. On one side the town occupied a spacious valley, farther away a widening yellow barren plain, a few pointy hills like mountains of sugar. At the end of the horizon, past the yellow stretch, and Sedona's desert rose, stood the dark blue thunder of San Francisco Peak. Next to the valley where the town rests, the serene Granite Mountain, which reminded me strongly of Sardinia's mountains. Looking to the opposite side, behind Thumb Butte, a green ocean of ponderosa pines, green, green, always green. Falcons spun like individual feathers, letting themselves be carried by the wind. I spent my time thinking, working on my poetry and songs, preparing for the beginning of college, for the orientation course: an intensive backpack trekking through forests and canyons of the Mogollon Rim.

I N THE SUMMER, WHEN all the other students were gone, my
shoes shuffled along the crumbled sidewalks in the afternoon
silence. The sun was a punch of light, a celestial oven asking
for every inch of my skin. Houses and public buildings slumbered
blissfully away in the fresh breeze of Prescott.

During the hot months, the square downtown was like a shady
room where the Court House stood as a white monolith. A small
crowd found shelter there; people rested against the roots of some
big tree while their dogs roamed about and parents improvised pic-
nics while their children ran on the wet grass. While the Europeans
strive toward a sort of elegance even when dressing casually, these
Americans took casual literally, showing off bitten hats, phosphorescent brims, socks under sandals, and the most bizarre chromatic
combination of shorts and t-shirts.

Even in that small town, we barely brushed one another; we
felt no obligation to ask a question of circumstance to each other.
What was diluting the communal sense? Maybe it was the silence
that billowed upon those streets, inviting everyone into soliloquies
or maybe it was the stillness that enveloped the houses upon the
hills high above the pavement as if everyone was living into his own
cloud where the wind blew and the city was a far reminiscence, a
muffled dream to be visited with respect on weekend evenings.

Time had built its nest on the cradle of these hills; there it
sat, dictating its limits and reassuring my sense of self. So did the
Sleeping Lion, The Thumb, The Sphinx, the Butte with as many
names as there are directions from where it can be seen. It stood
as a giant pin, holding time here, so to not let it escape beyond the

spinal cord of the mountains. There you entered in a planet of pines. A rustle sweet and remote whispered as down from the sky. It was the wind that came between the tall branches to recharge itself with aromas of wood and saps.

Julie Ann and I were thirsty for first-hand nature and for small-town traffic. Looking at the map, Prescott appeared between the green lakes of the national forest; it seemed safe from metropolitan urban sprawl. Yes, I had been thinking of national forests as triumphant safeguards of beauty. They had always inspired excitement in me since I was a child when my father took my brother and me for improvised trips into the greener regions of Italy: places like Parco Nazionale d'Abruzzo, Carpegna, Dolomiti and the smaller islands Giglio, D'Elba, Tremiti. Then, the "Parco Nazionale" was an opaque reign where I could find myself face-to-face with any of the animals and creatures I would see in books or heard in tales—wolves, bears, squirrels, deer, but maybe even the gnomes and fairies described in detail in some of my favorite books, those that made a science out of stories. Those forests were not definite places on the map, I could not believe they actually had boundaries and ended at some point; in my young mind, they were more like parallel dimensions where another sort of world could be entered.

Now I realized their limits, not only their physical ones but also the mental ones. The label National Forest or National Park or Wildlife Reserve developed a connotation of sadness for me. They entailed, and to some extent represented, the ecological ignorance and disability of our civilization. Children come into the world with a perfect ideal for everything and everyone and do not easily understand their own people can be doing harm to the beauty of the world. Upon realizing it, one separates from the group, from "them". In the struggle to find my place in society, to find my way back to a communal "us," I reconciled childhood's ideals with new-found knowledge of their discrepancy with reality. And so I began to long for a time when nature would no longer be under threat, for a humanity considering every inch of the world a reserve, for human life not to be in conflict with the wellbeing of plants, animals, and ecosystems, but rather benefit them, increasing the beauty and complexity of the natural world.

In our decision to relocate to Prescott, the nearby Arcosanti had played a role. A community that calls itself an "Urban Laboratory," a place that matched and re-inspired the ideal of city I held in my vision. Since the seventies, in Arcosanti, a group of people had been striving towards a prototype of a human community that may relate to the surrounding environment with intelligence and respect. The ideas Arcosanti still proposes are crucial for the well-being of our civilization, a valuable reservoir for the city planners of the future. Paolo Soleri, the architect and the founder, was Italian, from Turin, and he was still alive when we made Arizona home. When I drove to Cordes Junction, about an hour from Prescott, to spend part of the day between the surprising geometries of Arcosanti's walls and windows, the spatial rooms, the stairs and bridges, the complex roofs or just strolling up and down the paths between cypresses, I rediscovered a sense of kinship. For the one who has eyes to see it, Soleri's heritage is everywhere in Arcosanti. I went back to the vertical labyrinth of the Italian hill towns, where I played as a child, only this time, the town was on the edge of a canyon.

THE LETTERS TO MY family in Italy continued to flow, stitching together pieces of myself across thousands of miles. Often there were letters to my brother as if addressing a version of me who had not left, whom I loved now more than ever for his faithfulness and rootedness.

"In the evening, rooms turn red. It's the sign the bath of coolness is coming. I rest on my terrace. During days of clear sky the sunset may be a Latin love song or a French poem, but this evening it's a Sicilian field of oranges, and the horizon of hills is a backdrop of shadow puppets. The rock at the center holds now the nest of a few novel memories. If only you knew what a delight it is to begin to have memories here too. The new half of my present life acquires thickness, and that thirst of belonging finds a spring on which to quench itself.

"I've to open to a new childhood, to make space to a new language. Now that this new flesh begins to take form, I feel the pleasure of reconnecting with you again. I will continue to write, don't worry, change you with my changes."

I used letters like spells eluding space and time, stretching events, like a monsoon thunderstorm, carrying perception across the divide.

"The entire day, the sky pressed my thoughts against a void of warmth, like inside the giant oven of brushwood and clay of some enormous Indian ghost. Then, suddenly, out of the feverish dreams of the afternoon nap, a smell woke me.

"It's a smell of molten water and sand, aromas of cement and shrub, of sullied sky blue, of soil about to become rock and then held back and reborn soil, of washed mountain, of wild children ... After days of hesitation and false alarms, the Pack of Clouds has arrived in these desolated seas to let its roar vibrate in the marine space of the sky.

"My body is pervaded by a prehistoric calm, unknown to the mind and familiar to the blood, which exults behind the eyes when I turn upward towards great towers of cirri, white hot with light at the upper floors, confused and rubbed with darkness at the center, while they slide on the atmosphere.

"A venerable and phlegmatic thunder crumbles inexorable pushing these words, like straw flying all the way to you."

I sent letters to my mother sealing a new sense of belonging, as if to ask permission and absolution for giving myself to a new home.

"I don't know if it's because of the performance put up by the walls of a house that is finally ours, or of the warm colors that we have painted them with, or if it's because of the passing of time or of the hills and of the clear autumn air, or of the bicycle which I love to ride. Maybe it's all of these things that have brought my soul here, arriving always a bit after the body. So I now feel home. Once again I savor the hug of a small town: the sweet hues of hills in the bright tapestry of clouds, bizarre American houses like wheeling eagles, squared buildings and Mexicans squiggles, and cacti that I almost touch when riding my bike every day down to town, and howling of eternal and desperate thirst that keeps me awake a little longer in bed, nested with Julie Ann when we both keep silent and feel like happy and bewildered foreigners before getting lost in the jungle of dreams, and the last scene is the window, four or five stars, sometimes the moon."

THE ROARING FLAMES HAD come around May, swept thousands of acres, and burned down several houses. I stood one afternoon on the side of a hilly road near town observing the event together with a small crowd armed with cameras. The airplanes flew almost precipitating into the red flame tongues and burst clouds of red powder; the giant egg of the helicopters waved hanging from the sky until it was cracked, sending a shower to cool the world. Only the summer before, the flames riding fast winds over an arid landscape had reduced to ashes a good deal of Coconino, Tonto, and Sitgreaves National Forests across central Arizona. I remember returning home with a sensation of impotence. Like many others living near the forest did, I too considered the possibility of evacuation. What would I have taken with me? What would I leave? Differently from what happened in other parts of town, fires never touched the neighborhood of gray townhouses where we lived.

A few days after, we headed southwest through the National Forest within the Spruce Mountains. Hidden between trees, a maze of dirt roads spun itself around disused mines. On the sides of the main roads, log houses had been built and had been sold many times. In front of most of the homes hung sale signs, large clearings of ashes embraced sections of the road where skeletal trees raised prayers of carbon to the sky.

L IVING ON THE RAZOR of the Southwest requires careful attention to the climate; a simple mistake can cost you a great deal. During our first trips around Arizona, I bumped into my ignorance. We often failed to consider meeting extreme cold in preparing our bags: everyone knows that Arizona is a hot desert of cacti. Neither of us had read Joseph Wood Krutch warning that "seasons here are more a matter of vertical distance than of time" and especially that in this country "one is never at any season of the year far from a totally different climatic zone."

Once, during an unplanned excursion, mountain streets lured us higher and higher in a blind exploration, until we found ourselves driving along the Mogollon Rim right at the birth of autumn. The cold wind gusted out from below the cliff, howling through the thick pine forest ahead of us. In that late hour after the sunset, a dim light painted a blur of gray and brown all around. We looked for sticks to light a fire. That night, we put on all the clothing we had and tried to wrap our bodies as close to each other as we could. But the cold was so intense that any heat was stolen right out from our cocoon. The titanic gorge of the rim laid somewhere out there as the engine of the night, producing flaming cold spreading through the forest as through an unbreakable capillary system. We were tiny flies stuck in that web, defenseless prey to a spider of dry ice. We didn't sleep, rather we sort of hibernated or perhaps fainted for the useless and exhausting effort of holding on to those brief sparks of heat that the desperate clench of our bodies stingily generated. It was a gray night of vast and feverish dreams. In the morning it seemed even colder but the new light gave us the courage to break the thin crust of our chrysalis and jump inside the car with maximum heat on.

The shivering slowly diminished. In an hour or so we were driving down the mountain between crowds of saguaros in the slanted morning light. In Scottsdale, we stepped outside the car in a parking lot and we looked astounded at each other as the soothing warm air and the solid sunlight showered over us, melting the iciness off our muscles and bones.

AN APACHE STORY SAYS the earth was once too weak and needed bones; therefore, the four creators made rocky mountains. Indeed, when seeing the mountains sticking out of the California shore of the Colorado River, they immediately remind me of the bones of some giant or perhaps the broken glass of his oversized bottle. These rocks appear as worlds put aside the reach of man, like the distant bareness of the moon, a backdrop for existential pondering. Anyhow, places where you don't want to go barefooted.

Around the Lower Colorado people crowd to water like ants around honey. Several clusters of palms and RV parks explode along the drive toward Lake Havasu City, Arizona. The blue of the water is in utter contrast with the arid gray and brown of the rocks that menacingly rise everywhere on the way toward the town. "Havasu" means "blue waters" in the Mohave language. The soothing color is indeed an extract of the sky descended as angelic matter among us mortals.

Then, where a few decades ago there was nothing, like an enormous miracle, a city sprawled across the landscape. It is certainly a prime example of the stubborn ecological madness of the American urban paradigm. A tide of white houses has covered the Arizona side of the river; a tide regurgitated by a man's dream—Robert P. McCulloch's. His dream has now stemmed into and through a myriad of other men's and women's thirsty dreams and gained a life of its own. McCulloch, a businessman who made his fortune in the oil industry and in designing and producing engines, searched for a testing site for his beloved nautical motors, and finding the shores of the Lower Colorado River irresistible, he had the vision of a prosperous city, a lake oasis. He then bought the largest lot of land at that time ever sold in Arizona and started an intensive advertisement campaign offering free flights from all over the country to his future city for prospective buyers.

The closest that you can get to the ocean in Arizona is Lake Havasu City. Here, you have the sound of waves, smell of algae, water-crafts, sand and rocky beaches, and cliché postcard bikini girls. But especially watercrafts, of all shapes and colors: jet boats, ski boats, and pontoon boats that cruise the cool river waters while a similar panoply of aircraft roar through the sky. Surely it is not a coincidence that McCulloch loved motors above anything else and that he used to say that the best moments of his life were his successes in boat racing. On these shores he planned and constructed a motor paradise. Maybe it is useful to wonder what would have happened to this place if McCulloch's heart would have been set on something else other than the motor, let's say chess, bird watching, or why not kites ...

Apparently in McCulloch's mind Lake Havasu had an unforgivable fault: the lack of history. But he wasn't patient enough to wait a few centuries so he looked around for other solutions. The only way to inject his newly born city with hormones of history and to have it stand in front of the world's eyes as a place worthy of visiting was to buy a good dose of already made ruins. I could not believe my eyes when I saw, driving into Lake Havasu City, a massive elaborate bridge connecting the main shore with somewhere in the midst of the Colorado River. It is a European bridge, specifically a late nineteenth century one equipped with elegant lamp posts. I had driven hours through the desert of Southwestern America to stand in front of the London Bridge. A nice surprise since at the time I had not yet been to London.

McCulloch bought this bridge from the home of the Big Ben when it was decided to build a new one in its place. The bridge was dismantled, each piece numbered, and shipped to the coast of California and then trucked to Lake Havasu City. Since there wasn't a reason for a bridge there, McCulloch also cut a canal, making the Lake Havasu City peninsula into an island. If the bridge had a soul, would it be missing the streets and buildings it used to connect, the cold and the rain, the European crowd? "London Bridge goes to America" would surely make for a moving children's book title. In October 1971, the bridge was opened to its new company of pedestrians. I really wish I could have been there.

Pulled by an irresistible curiosity to get closer to that displaced piece of Britain, I parked near its entrance where four lion statues are spraying water into a large fountain and several toy-buildings emanate English flavor. Two plastic-like columns greeted me to the English Village, Land of London. Where the bridge casts its large shadow a teeming world of hybrid European elements has blossomed: small restaurants with outside seating, ice cream stalls, medieval pinnacles, souvenir shops, a double-decker bus, and other specimens. While a human fauna worthy of Venice Beach gets tanned on boats and sips cold beer, across the vaults of the cold big bricks of the London Bridge can be spotted the arid Mountains of the Chemehuei Indian Reservation. Taken by the effulgence of this cultural minestrone, fruit of some groundbreaking genetic experiment between California, England, and Arizona, I stood for long moments pondering while my notions about how a place defines itself from another became more and more murky.

Lake Havasu City, as do other cities among which Las Vegas stands as queen, is a polyphony that sings the voice of the world's complexity, a patchwork of empty shells there only to recall for you something with their superficial presence. And indeed, it is truly a titillating experience when all the stories you may know on the London Bridge, the Chemehuei Indians, the Lower Colorado, Arizona, McCulloch, California beaches and whatever you can fit there begin pollinating one another.

McCulloch's mind was fertile with desires. When death took him, he was busy attempting to accomplish a new vision. It was a hybrid combination between a helicopter and an airplane, the easy-to-fly aircraft for every Lake Havasu City citizen's garage; it could have taken off from the driveway. It seems that McCulloch's vision had a lot to do with the experience of nature from motorized perspective, or in one word, with comfort.

I paid a few dollars extra for a room with one of those spectacular views the tourist brochures prescribed. I lay in a wide taut bed, alternating my head from the sixty-channel cable TV to the calm Colorado waters darkening with the evening across the wall-window. And I have to say that I felt grateful to old McCulloch for thinking of me; it was there I forgave him for the imperfections of his vision.

That evening, in the third-floor room of the hotel, our gazes fixed toward the sunset, a sultry and orange sun that melted as butter on those searing peaks in the horizon. And as the day was pulled to a conclusion, with that rare flavor of death, the world stretched in its last opportunity for complete joy. While the sun submerged itself, our bodies trembled with nostalgic desire.

CLINGING TO A HILL as a colony of termites, I could imagine the tiny creatures' daily dramas: emotional, drunk, armed, digging and carrying rocks up to their king dwelling in the palace from where he watches them with an inscrutable gaze. Copper, zinc, silver, and gold is what feeds his vast hunger. The working creatures get back all they are supposed to need and desire: women for sex and whiskey for everything else.

William Andrew Clark, with the determined crystalline eyes worthy of the Joan of Arc portrait that he admired in the panels of his one hundred and twenty-one room and thirty-one bathroom Gothic mansion in New York City, was since 1888 the first king termite of Jerome, Arizona. Two times per year, he rolled with his private wagon train all the way across the States to Jerome to check on the copper camp that made him a millionaire. Jerome was his secret, and he let none talk about its splendors outside its borders.

"King" Clark's monopoly came to an end when James Douglas, a mining expert working for Phelps-Dodge, and his astute son "Rawhide" Jimmy Douglas managed to acquire a mine below Jerome hill, by then known as Cleopatra Hill. The Douglases spent a huge amount of money in the first two years with no success, but, in 1914, their Little Daisy mine revealed the largest body of pure ore ever found in American mining and began making a profit of about one million dollars per month. The two kings of Jerome struggled with one another, and mineworkers could easily exploit the situation for their benefit, asking for higher wages and better work conditions.

Sitting outside Jimmy Douglas's white adobe mansion, I could see the Verde Valley opening one hundred-eighty degrees in front of me with its reddish sandstone fortifications beyond waves strewn with bushes. Today, besides being a touristic ghost town, Jerome also has a reputation as an artists' town. The view extending from the "J" hill toward Sedona makes a fancy window-wall to several art studios and shops. The complex hues of this landscape, relentlessly smeared by sky and sun, change drastically with every passing minute. For the crowds of painters and photographers who stop here, justly representing this scenery is a tall task.

On the other side of Douglas's home, now a historical state park, I could spot the Little Daisy Hotel standing as a beautiful empty shell. Close by are some nice homes once belonging to mine executives and a blue villa built by James Douglas as a wedding gift for his son. As I look over the old town from here, I struggle to imagine this place vibrating with multitudes of people, fifteen thousand at its peak, buzzing with the hopes of rich futures.

This was one of the richest settlements in Arizona, where the most expensive and luxurious hotels were found. It was the shopping center of the Verde Valley, with opera houses, countless saloons and Chinese restaurants. Jerome was considered a "tough town", "Arizona's Sodom and Gomorrah." It wasn't a safe place to be for a man of law, and the stories of killing and gun fighting are many and colorful, nor for prostitutes who catered to drunk and over-worked miners in the town's many brothels.

But only a tiny portion of Jerome can be seen by the tourist passing through; there is also another invisible underworld. It was arduous to perceive the vastness of the tunnels and shaft systems that spread underneath my feet, or all the barrels of darkness rolling throughout the mining tunnels reaching down as far as 4,500 feet. Below is another city, a creature much larger, ingenious, and terrible, buried up to its face. The town above, merely a mask to conceal the ugly grimace of many a miner's pain.

The son of the first king, William Clark, Charlie, eventually managed his father's mine. He is remembered as a man obsessed with women, fast horses, and high stakes poker. After his father's death, in the late twenties, in the attempt to reach a good body of ore directly underneath the town, he used hundreds of thousands of tons of dynamite. But the bet was too high. The explosion dislodged the bedrock supporting Jerome and caused part of the historic town to begin sliding. Some of the richest buildings slid down the cliff. The termites' thirst has devoured the colony as well. The mine was exhausted by 1938 and since the big explosion, the houses of Jerome hang over the cliff as an aerial Atlantis waiting to crumble at the feet of Cleopatra Hill.

O N EASTER DAY, JULIE ANN and I left for a picnic in Sedona. We turned on a dirt road following a sign for the archeological site of Palatki. The earth was red and sparked an exalting contrast with the green bushes and cobalt sky. Driving in a cloud of dust we reached a gulf of rounded rocks—crimson pilasters worked by a tropical sea around 300 million years ago. Subterranean streams fed a thick velvet of grass and shrubs. Under the smooth walls, secluded by trees, rest the ruins of an old village. A half-a-mile walk away, a caved portion of the cliff contains a Sistine Chapel of pictographs.

The dwellings at Palatki are supposed to have been built by the Sinagua, a farming people living in central Arizona about a thousand years ago, while the pictographs present various historic phases of prehistoric Indian culture. Each of them used a different pigment to draw on these walls, perhaps to distinguish themselves from the previous ones or to preserve and understand them. The ranger tells us that the red abstract symbols belonged to archaic cultures dating back to an astounding six thousand BCE, the hunter and gatherers of the Archaic period. Then come the yellow artworks of the farming Sinagua and after them the black drawings of Yavapai and Apache.

Among the Palatki pictographs I saw dwarf deer, some of which had long tails that rose up in the sky and exploded like firecrackers. Women seemed to give birth to strange beasts. Dark ladders extended upward. Men flew across the ceiling head down. Circles and spirals penetrated the stone. Between the pictographs were drawn two entwined hearts, supposedly belonging to two fond members of the Anglo families who settled this area at the beginning of the twentieth century. The locals claim their own New Age interpretations for some of these images, finding parallels and similarities with Eastern symbols and looking for spiritual doorways in the stone. These ambiguous traces still call us back and continue to inspire new tales, which in turn reveal who we are today perhaps more than who we were then. We return to the car reawakened, our presence more pronounced against the vast backdrop of colors.

WHEN I WAS ABOUT sixteen I was taken by a feverish yearning for nature's infinitude. I constantly looked for a chance to hike up any of the hills around my Cesena to stare into the horizon or up into night space. Sometimes describing piece by piece the marvel of such intricacy and vastness to a friend, sometimes in my journal. I privileged high lookouts either natural or manmade because what I needed was in essence amplitude. I struggled to feel more of my smallness as well as to contain more of that largeness; the earth seemed to lift me up and the center of my mind fly open. With eyes shut I could feel the space.

Then, years later, in the deep Southwest of America, I found myself scanning the evolution of the planet in the vertical timeline of the Grand Canyon with my gaze, infinity meeting eternity. I rafted through the Colorado River's gelid waters in late fall with a group of fellow students. The last night of the trip, having by then passed all rapids, we attached the boats together and kept navigating slowly towards Lake Mead. That night my eyes closed while dark walls of stones glided by in a continuum of patterns and shades. As a horizontal kaleidoscope of the universe, moved by the steady hand of the river, the inscrutable bowels of the planet unfolded. For that night, I rested my life on the corner of the universe, and as on the day of my death, I had it all together.

I wish I could fully convey that timeless smoothness, that cryptic coloration, that imperturbable coldness, and the thought spurred by that view. And above all, I wish I could explain the reason why that profound mineral gorge has an affinity for death. Many have been dragged into a meditation about mortality in staring transfixed into the layers of the Grand Canyon. Henry Miller, on his way to California, once saw the representative of all human activity about to slip into extinction in the page of a comic book lying on the edge of the canyon. The religious experiences of moving beyond manhood are numerous in the literature about the Southwest, to the point that we may think of some spots as sort of churches or better as temples of the universe.

When I stepped under the shadow of another Arizona wonder, the Tonto natural bridge, and I looked up into the pale vault where confused echoes enlarged and lost themselves, I was reminded of Saint Peter's cathedral in Rome and its cooling marbles. Even there, in the summer, after the grueling voyage through the scorching dehydrating metropolis, the bastion of the Catholic faith is reached with dazzled eyes and with a thirst for shade deep in the skin. The religion of this natural cathedral has been reverberating forever. Its liturgies rhyme with my genes and its bas-relief retrace the logic of my veins.

On the crags that compose the canyon, the sheer green vegetation of trees and cacti appears to take dramatic poses as if "shrinking back in awe" as Charles Lummis described it more than a hundred years ago. When Lummis visited the Tonto Natural Bridge, it wasn't yet a state park and in the green valley above, in place of the luxurious gift shop was the modest barrack of David Gowan Goodfellow. This was a prospector who stumbled across the bridge during his explorations and claimed squatter's rights over the surrounding area. When Charles and his companions descended the valley, David appeared to them a cheerful hermit who loved to play with his cat and rooster. David, the hermit, considered this "his bridge," on top of which he had an orchard of peach trees. He must have choked himself with beauty spending so many years in this solitary church.

As I lay in a rounded chair-like rock formation cooling myself in the absolute shadow of six billion cubic yards of travertine, my eyes were kidnapped by the effulgence of strings of water raining down from a kind of brilliant stalactite of green and vanilla hues.

The water descending was taken like threads between the fingers of the sun.

Suddenly, I didn't know what I would have given to have Julie Ann and her warmth there close to me in that cold timeless chamber. Instead, my body seated there like a drop of flesh amidst chatter of echoing sounds taken in by the arch of that hollow universe as in a photograph from another planet. About ten years after Charles Lummis's visit, David Gowan would persuade his family to come to join him from Scotland and settle the land.

O THER PATHS WERE AWAITING me, long detours in Indiana and Connecticut, building the case of my profession as a bridge-builder, securing new cables between Italy and America. It was a long and necessary hiatus, seven years filled with uncertainty and ice, learning and sacrifice, clinging to the old hopes we had dreamt in the cool desert nights of Arizona.

Probably only southwestern soil could nourish my seeds, and I was eventually drawn back, as a sign of fate, this time to Southern California, to a deceivingly small town called Orange, on the edge of Los Angeles's sprawl, pressed against the Santa Ana mountains, to take a post as professor of Italian. I recall flying over the desert lands for the first time after so long, recognizing from the airplane the road home, the mountains of New Mexico, the painted desert, the Colorado River, the Grand Canyon, remembering the poetic enigma that elements acquire in the desolation of space.

My heart jumped at every thought of returning southwest. I felt protected and on the right path. Life responded to me again, the theater of human appearance appeared for what it was, meaningful yet inconsequential, like traces of words on sand, the smaller something was the grander its significance.

Amidst a spirited community of humanists, artists and scientists called Chapman University, Julie Ann and I fully entered into the great river of our vocations, riding our dreams' big waves, completely blinded, and in tune. It was as if we mirrored each other, us and that strange land of California. With all its problems and potentials, California was capable of containing our thirst for change. It showed us clearly how we had lived life in the wake of our visions, romantically, choosing adventure over security, leaving Italy for America, Dallas for Arizona, Prescott for Indiana and then Connecticut, and Orange County. It was clear that our capacity for aspiration had been both our curse and our gasoline.

After many years now, it still feels like we are on one of those early trips southwest, Julie Ann and I, with snacks heated by the sun waiting in the car, itineraries to return to, stories to decipher, a vision to grasp, inexorable restlessness. And from under the pages of our southwestern story, our little Sofia was born, dream made incarnate.

S OFIA LOVES JUNKYARDS: THE possibilities they store, the re-
demption awaiting all things, a world deconstructed is finally
perceivable in new ways. The first time I took her to the Watts
Towers, I felt that I was showing her something that she could
have concocted herself; her young eyes immediately entranced by
it. Hidden in the gray dusty carpet of Los Angeles, encased with
bright glass, tin, objects of all sorts, rise bejeweled spikes made of
shiny lost specks of America.

Sabato Rodia, the inconspicuous and wild man who erected
them of his own accord on his plot of land in Watts, a town scarred
by poverty, racial tensions and rioting, had arrived in his teens with
his brother from the Italian village of Serino at the foot of the
Picentini Mountains in the Campania region. After a mine took
his brother in Pennsylvania, and after Sabato's failed attempts to
create a new family in the West, he began his work on the towers
in 1920. At the same time, back East, Italian immigrants were
erecting the modern skyline of New York City, dreaming the
New World while also being devoured by it, crucified by danger-
ous working conditions, prejudice, and financial hardships, as the
writer Pietro di Donato would narrate in his feverish 1939 novel
Christ in Concrete.

Rodia referred to his towers with the Spanish name Nuestro
Pueblo, calling to mind the adobe settlements of New Mexico, only
this time, the desert from which to take shelter was the urban wilderness of Los Angeles. Yet, his construction, which took about
twenty five years to complete, was often vandalized; eventually,
Sabato Rodia left Watts, never to return. Still the towers stand, now

protected for their unique beauty and symbolic power, a sanctuary for art and hope.

Five-year-old little Sofia is tracing her fingers on the colorful fragments that emerge unexpectedly from the concrete, like the shells she once found inside the walls of the city of Lecce in the heel of the Italian peninsula. I can't help but muse about the story of each one of those fragments, while also guess at the design that they form together, their preserved diversity and expanding unity. I know that Sofia is also looking for handholds, because in her mind this sort of thing can only be made for climbing, for reaching the pinnacle; at other times, she explores how that wonder could turn into her home. And now that I think of it, it was after Watts that she started asking for the gift of a junkyard of her own, perhaps to erect, like Sabato, her unique sign of existence, to be finally made visible, to flower.

WHERE SOME DECADES AGO was all farms and orchards, now stand shimmering shopping malls, luxurious theaters, towering crystals of office buildings. Much of this crop is tied to the delicate lima bean, the treasure of the Swedish Segerstrom family's expansive farm of Costa Mesa. The bean, or better its spirit, is remembered now as one of the elements of Isamu Noguchi's Garden, the *California Scenario*. Massive beans of granite are piled together in a corner of the garden, their purity and value is what allowed for the greatest of the fruits, art, to flourish, through the wide reach of the Segerstroms' patronage. Noguchi's garden, primeval and futuristic, manifest and ethereal, is a playground of memory. It is an experience returning our attention to the foundations, to the voices of different biomes, to the abundant employability of renewable energies, to our responsibility in making choices about the land. The attention in question belongs to those who we can trust will always be present to their senses, children.

Little Sofia would not leave the garden, neither would I. On a sunny Sunday morning of a weirdly sultry fall, as if still searing from the summer's wildfires, architect friends took us here as a respite from the isolation of the pandemic. After another week of surreal online schooling, of undesired solitude, of perturbing news, we came to this consonance of sounds, colors, shapes, to the clear simplicity of an affirmative destiny. The Segerstrom family used its fortune well, and so did Noguchi use his talent. He did so by following his mother's advice to take night classes at the Leonardo da Vinci Art School in the Lower East Side of Manhattan, where Onorio Ruotolo, "The Rodin of Little Italy", another emigrated artist from the inland of Naples, like Rodia, introduced him to sculpting. Noguchi let the suffering of his own Japanese-American experience, what has perhaps been the hardest chapter of that history during WWII, open his heart and direct his discipline. He discovered an organic balance between points of inspiration distant in time and space, to be employed to benefit all through public work and mass production.

Noguchi's legacy includes many gardens and playgrounds that seem to speak the universal grammar of children. By seeing Sofia's immediate bond with the Costa Mesa garden, I sense that Noguchi must have also thought of the parallel between lima beans and children. Certainly a harsh life can render children like overcooked lima beans, bitter and sulfurous. Yet inside both is stored a delicate sweetness, like desire or hope, a strength that must be harnessed for the future. Because children are another element of the *California Scenario*, another source of humanity; they are the spring that splits the mountain of pure Carrara marble on the map of time.

I N MY DREAMS THERE exists a direct passage between Italy and the American Southwest.

I'm strolling through the historic center of Rome, discovering the city as I had when I was twenty. It opens in front of me with its most glorious Elysian Fields, large boulevard until the eye can see, symmetries of fountains surround me. The miracle of a city as a gigantic work of art, the transcendent achievement of citizenship simmered through the centuries, my utter exhilaration for it forming a bright scar deep within me.

But suddenly some newly arisen task requires me to cross the metropolitan cosmos, and the only way through is via a score of *mezzi*, which in the dream I know to be more than public vehicles, a means to something, intermediaries between ideas and reality.

The dream shifts to a series of trams, trolleybuses, subway trains, all that the city offers to reach the promised goal.

However, the promise soon reveals itself a lie, a doomed ambition. But rather than despair, the slowing down of my design opens into a pleasing digression filled with new promises for the senses, like breaking into a new alley or into a new conversation with someone different, gifting myself a great meal in a dusty one-room tavern.

Until a way through becomes known, a shortcut that has survived from another phase of the city's urban development. A mono-syllabic bus conductor notifies me of the right stop, which strangely coincides with a forced entrance into an embassy-like hotel hall.

Inside, I repeat once again my query and a pair of nonplussed attendants point me through a corridor toward an elevator. I do as

I'm told and am stunned at realizing that it's actually an old and dark mine shaft, where the elevator itself is a sturdy and tattered seat in which I apprehensively begin to buckle myself. One of the attendants notices my concern and confirms that the seat will bring me where I need to go, though they don't seem to have experienced this route personally and can't tell me much about how it works. I ask how long the drop takes, the answer is only a few hours, I freeze, but this is, after all, the prescribed way in the city's plans. The attendant slowly places the seat in position and I'm in.

I slide down a dimly lighted tunnel at increasing speed, struggling to control my shaggy pod. I go through many waves of emotions and trains of thoughts during the drop. Strangely, it seems internally endless and at the same time externally immediate. After an entire journey of the mind, which is though only a handful of minutes, I'm suddenly there.

The scene fades into a new one where I'm being driven by a kind, optimistic, even though slightly naive professor to a large warehouse playfully colored with pink and yellow stripes in the evening dusk. I make out the large letters on the front of the redeemed building: Prescott College West.

Awake, my rational mind draws its conclusions: the uniqueness of Italy and my own deep bond with the beauty of its spacious living room; the curse of Italian adulthood with its aimless joy like a rolling carpet parading one invisibly through the social scene; the serendipitous and inescapable path to somewhere, America; the unnerving and mysterious ride to professional realization; my new workplace as the continuation of my quest for true Education; and probably more. My bridge between Italy and the American Southwest feels now just like a passing dream—surprisingly personal, mildly disappointing, strangely liberating.

W E DEPART, THE THREE of us, to flee from the compulsive bubble of a self-imposed lockdown. We travel fast inside our silver capsule, skirting the Santa Ana mountains and squeezing through the bottleneck of the San Gorgonio Pass, along with countless other human blood cells, flowing in and out of the great atrium of the Los Angeles Basin. We brought with us stories to unwrap, like snacks for the trip, for Sofia to sink her young teeth into, while the earth's skin changes its light all around us from perfect green to browns, from yellow to almost white.

Outside the embrace of the saintly peaks, where deserts meet, unworldly beauty, unimaginable loneliness, humanity's shards abandoned and reinvented. In the overpowering windy night, some of them endure inside scattered huts thrown about like boats in a storm. Others manifest their subjective dream inside a metal fence at the margin of nowhere, touchingly honest and inescapably naive, ridiculous, and monstrous—the desert shaking us to the root of our being. And in the distance, where the miraculous peaks harness humidity, hope awaits, and to it we will flock again, dutifully lining up, without end.

In the middle of the night, out of reach of the day's rapaciousness, life's story comes to the surface. The trajectory unearthed beneath this imagined journey whispers wild plans of movements southwest, to new lands, perhaps to find myself one day on the other side, into a reversed boot in the middle of the sea. This enduring spin of mind preserves my eye awakened from the tyranny of habit provides the illusory wood that feeds my flame. May I forever move, in space or in spirit, and may I forever move southwest, towards mirages in the desert, the next green hill, the delusion of paradise.

About the Author

FEDERICO PACCHIONI is a scholar, writer, and educator. Born in Italy, he has traveled both the Italian peninsula and the United States extensively, and currently lives in Orange, California. A professor of Italian Studies at Chapman University, he is author and co-author of volumes of Italian cultural history such as: *Inspiring Fellini: Literary Collaborations behind the Scenes* (University of Toronto Press, 2014), *A History of Italian Cinema* (Bloomsbury Academic Press, 2017), and *The Image of the Puppet in Italian Theater, Literature and Film* (Metauro Editore, 2020 and Palgrave Macmillan, 2022); as well as creative works, including two collections of poetry: *La paura dell'amore* (Raffaelli Editore, 2014) and *I frutti del mio giardino* (Manni Editori, 2022).

Printed in May 2022
by Gauvin Press,
Gatineau, Québec